PARENTAL UNEMPLOYMENT

Ellen Wijnberg

RSVP
RAINTREE
STECK-VAUGHN
PUBLISHERS
The Steck-Vaughn Company

Austin, Texas

Consultants:
Kathleen M. DeCato, Clinical Supervisor; Family Service Association
   of Bucks County, PA
Phyllis Macklin, Independent Career Consultant; East Windsor, NJ
Lori Myrick Creighton, Counselor; Liberty Middle School, Madison, AL

Developed for Steck-Vaughn Company by Visual Education Corporation, Princeton, New Jersey
Project Director: Jewel Moulthrop
Editors: Dale Anderson, Paula McGuire
Editorial Assistant: Carol Ciaston
Photo Research: Cindy Cappa

Raintree Steck-Vaughn Publishers staff
Editor: Gina Kulch
Project Manager: Joyce Spicer
Electronic Production: Scott Melcer
Photo Editor: Margie Foster

Library of Congress Cataloging-in-Publication Data
Wijnberg, Ellen, 1952-
      Parental unemployment / Ellen Wijnberg.
         p.   cm. — (Teen hot line)
      Includes index.
      Summary: Discusses what happens when a teenager's parent loses his or her job, the effect on the family especially with regard to finances, and how the teenager can help out.
      ISBN:0-8114-3525-3
      1. Unemployment — Psychological aspects — Juvenile literature.
      2. Unemployed — Psychology — Juvenile literature.   3. Parent and child — Juvenile literature.   [1. Unemployment.]   I. Title. II. Series.
      HD5708.W54   1994
      331.13'7'019—dc20
                                                                    93-25154
                                                                    CIP   AC

Photo Credits: Cover: © Gabe Palmer/The Stock Market; **15:** © Michael Newman/ PhotoEdit; **16:** David M. Grossman/Photo Researchers, Inc.; **25:** Robert Fox/Impact Visuals; **29:** © Tony Freeman/PhotoEdit; **31:** Margaret Thompson/The Picture Cube; **33:** ©Michael Newman/PhotoEdit; **40:** Aneal Vohra/Unicorn Stock Photos; **43:** Elena Rooraid/PhotoEdit; **44:** © Unicorn Stock Photos; **52:** Michael Newman/ PhotoEdit; **56:** © Robert W. Ginn/PhotoEdit; **63:** Ulrike Welsch/ PhotoEdit; **64:** Myrleen Ferguson/PhotoEdit; **67:** Mary Kate Denny/Photo Researchers, Inc.

Printed and bound in the United States

1 2 3 4 5 6 7 8 9 0 LB 99 98 97 96 95 94

CONTENTS

What the
Teen
Hot Line
Is All About

This book is like a telephone hot line. It answers questions you have about your parent's unemployment and its effect on you. In answering your questions, we will present some facts about unemployment and some suggestions for how you can deal with your family's situation. Many families across the country are experiencing the unemployment of one or both parents. But the problems, solutions, and coping strategies will be different for each family. We will discuss some of the most common problems that teens have in dealing with their parent's unemployment. You can use the suggestions that best fit your special situation. Think of us as the voice on the phone, always there to answer your questions, even the ones that are hard to ask.

Just so you know why we're here, we've prepared a list of some of the issues discussed in this book.

1 Your parent's unemployment as part of a larger economic picture.

2 Keeping the lines of communication between you and your parents open at this difficult time.

3 The effects of your parent's unemployment on you and your family and what you can do to make things better for yourself—starting right now!

4 Changes in your family's financial picture and your own money needs.

5 Moving to a new place and what you can do to make the move, if necessary, less painful.

6 Learning about the job-search process and what you can do to help.

7 Special issues, such as divorce, alcohol and drug abuse, and family violence, that may develop as a result of the job loss.

We'll also tell you how to get help if these, or other problems, are occurring in your family.

After you've read the book, we hope that you will discover some answers to the questions that you have about your parent's unemployment. We hope this book will help you cope with the painful and confusing feelings you may be experiencing. And we hope you will use the suggestions and resources you find in this book to begin to find solutions to your problems.

Remember that this book is just a start; no book, or friend, or counselor—no matter how helpful—can change your life. That is up to you. Thinking about the issues raised in this book is an important step toward taking control of your life.

Interview

Kyle is 15 and the eldest of three brothers. His family had a comfortable life in the suburbs of a major city—until his father, a landscaper, lost his job. Kyle described the changes that occurred as a result of his dad's unemployment.

Before my dad lost his job we had a pretty good life. I mean, we weren't rich or anything, but I guess we weren't poor either. My dad worked in landscaping. He put trees and things in people's lawns, things like that. He worked for the same company for as long as I can remember. Then he lost his job. I was in shock, no lie. I mean, I never thought that something like that could happen to us. Afterwards, I thought about it, and I said to myself, "Hey stupid, unemployment is all they talk about on the news. Why is this such a shock?" You just never think it will happen to you, man. I mean, it's like getting hit by a car it happens to . . . other people, but you just don't think it's going to happen to you.

I think Dad must have been pretty out of it, too. He didn't freak or yell; he didn't cry. But it's like he just was in shock . . . all quiet. He just seemed to sit and stare at the wall. It was very spooky. I mean Dad is usually . . . the way he used to be, I mean . . . he's usually really active. He watched football and sports stuff with his friends. He was always having barbecues and just hangin' with his friends. And then after he lost his job . . . his friends didn't seem to come to the house anymore . . . and Dad didn't go out. It was like he was a nobody.

My mom changed, too. She and Dad didn't seem to laugh anymore. We always used to joke around a lot at our house. And that kind of thing stopped. Sometimes I would start one of our jokes with Dad, but he wouldn't pick up on it. It was like he wasn't my dad. He was more like some alien that looked like Dad but didn't have his personality. Mom wasn't too much fun either.

My dad started looking for a new job, but that didn't seem to go too well. I tried to talk to Dad about it, but he didn't want to talk. I waited until I could talk to Mom alone, and then I asked her what was going on. Mom told me to "give Dad time," time, man! She said it was pretty bad right now. She said that construction was down . . . that they weren't building anything, and that Dad's work was tied to that, so there weren't many jobs in landscaping right now. She said that the people who had landscaping jobs weren't giving them up and there weren't any new jobs. And if there was an opening, that lots of people . . . too many people . . . applied for the job.

I guess I just never thought about any of this before. Our life had this routine. I mean sometimes I used to think it was boring, but now looking back, it was kind of cool that you could tell just how things were going. Dad always got his paycheck on Fridays. He'd come home and pick us up—me and my little brothers, my mom—and we'd all go out to dinner. Nothing fancy, I mean Mickey D's, or pizza, or something like that . . . but you can forget that now. I mean, the other night we had cereal for dinner, cereal, man. I don't want to sound like I'm complaining; I mean I'm not starving or anything, but cereal for dinner . . . not the way things used to be. Mom cooked a lot, and there'd always be people at the house—Dad's friends, Mom's friends, or her sisters . . . they practically lived at our house. There would be so many people when we sat down to dinner.

Now people hardly come over. I don't really know why . . . like if Dad said, "Don't come over" or something, or if it just kind of happened. But it's real quiet now, and sad and spooky. I think maybe it's because our house used to be fun, and now it's not.

So now Mom works. She never did before. I used to think Dad was kind of old-fashioned because he had this pride thing, like, "My wife won't work." and I always thought, what's the matter with a woman working? But with Dad it was this caveman . . . Tarzan thing. But then, Dad just didn't get a job so Mom went out looking for work. Dad said it was easier for her because she could get a lower paying job, but he wanted something more because he was the breadwinner. I don't really understand why he couldn't go for some kind of job like my mom ended up getting; she does checkout at the supermarket. But Dad let me know that he wasn't really going to talk about this whole thing too much. So mostly I just let him talk whenever he was ready to.

Things are very weird now. Mom is working and Dad is home all day. He says that he's going to start his own car repair business, and there's usually some kind of car in front of the house that he's working on. But I don't think he's pulling in too much bread. I don't really ask because of how touchy he gets, but I don't think people are paying him much to fix up these old heaps.

Before, we lived in an apartment, but it was kind of like having a house. We had the top floor of a two-family house. Now we still live in the same house, but we had to move into the downstairs apartment that's much smaller. I sleep in a bedroom with my two brothers, which is something I could have lived without. My one brother isn't so bad, but the other is a real neat freak, and he's always screaming at me about ridiculous things like I left my socks on the floor or something. We've gotten into it a few times, and I sort of beat him up. We never got along that great because he's a real pain, but things weren't this bad before.

I hope things change soon, but I can't see anything great happening real soon. I don't think Mom's job pays really enough for us to live on, because I heard Mom and Dad discussing moving to an even smaller apartment the other day. I can't imagine that because things are so cramped now. My dad sold his car and got a really old used one. I guess they used up any money they had in the bank, if they had any, so I don't think that there's any other way of getting some money. So probably we will have to move again.

I don't think I'm ever going to get married. I mean, I guess I will because it seems like that's what you're sup-posed to do, but I never want to be in my dad's shoes . . . a family and no job, no money.

I hope my dad gets a real job, but I don't know when that will happen or if it will ever happen. And even if he does, life will never go back to the way it was . . . too much stuff has happened, man, too much bad stuff.

BULLETIN BOARD

National unemployment is defined as the number of people in our country who are willing and able to work, but who are not currently working. Here are some facts and figures about the national employment/unemployment picture.

1992 Unemployment Statistics

Number of employed people in United States: 118.3 million

Number of unemployed people in United States: 9.3 million

Percent of total population: 7.3%

Percent of total population last year: 7.7%

Single-Parent/Dual-Parent Families (1991)

Number of U.S. families with at least one family member fully employed: 49.8 million

Number of U.S. families with children under 18, in which at least one parent is unemployed: 2.5 million

Percent of single-parent families with one working family member: 44%

Percent of two-parent families with at least one working family member: 80%

Duration of Unemployment

Number of people unemployed for 15 weeks or less: decreasing

Number of people unemployed for 15 weeks or more: increasing

Finding a Job

The five most common ways to look for work are:

- Using a public employment agency
- Using a private employment agency
- Contacting employers directly
- Contacting friends or relatives
- Answering classified ads

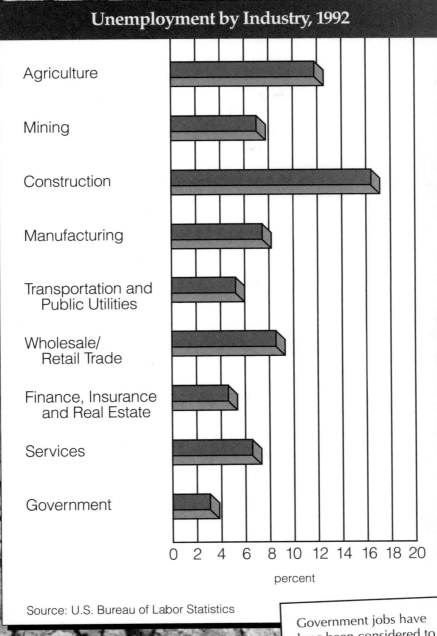

Unemployment by Industry, 1992

Industry	
Agriculture	
Mining	
Construction	
Manufacturing	
Transportation and Public Utilities	
Wholesale/Retail Trade	
Finance, Insurance and Real Estate	
Services	
Government	

0 2 4 6 8 10 12 14 16 18 20

percent

Source: U.S. Bureau of Labor Statistics

Sources: Career Information Center. Macmillan, 1993.
Monthly Labor Review. Bureau of Labor Statistics,
    U.S. Department of Labor, December, 1992.
Statistical Abstracts of the United States, 1992. U.S.
    Department of Commerce.

Government jobs have long been considered to be the most stable. The construction industry, however, is one of the first to feel the effects of a recession.

CHAPTER 1

Communicating

Q My name is Dave and I'm 15 years old. My dad lost his job, and now it seems like my whole family is falling apart. Dad and Mom fight all the time, and my brother sulks alone in his room. It seems like Mom and Dad's answer to everything is, "We can't afford it." I'm worried about what's going to happen. I don't know what to do and feel scared a lot and angry, too. Please help.

A Dave, what you are going through is rough. You are not alone, however. Many families across the country are facing the unemployment problem. When a parent becomes unemployed, it affects the whole family. Your dad has an unemployment problem, and his problem is causing you to have problems. You can't solve his problem. That is beyond your control. But you may be able to help during this family crisis. And the first step is to try to talk to your parents about it.

• • • • • • • • • • •

Q You don't understand. You just can't approach my parents about anything these days.

Besides, they've never talked to me about family finances and stuff like that. I'm just a kid. I wouldn't know where to begin to talk to them about this.

A Well, you might begin by letting them know that you are concerned about the family situation and want to take part in making things better for everybody. And this means that you must first make an active decision about sharing the family's burdens as well as their comforts. This may mean taking on some new responsibilities and making some sacrifices. You have to decide whether you want to help as much as you can or whether you'd be more comfortable letting things work out for themselves. Some young people find it very difficult to deal with their parents' problems in a direct way.

• • • • • • • • • • • •

 Well, sure I'd like to help. I love my parents, but I'm scared they'll be angry if I start interfering with their problems.

A Sharing their problems is not the same as interfering. They're lucky parents to have a kid ready to help out in a crisis.

• • • • • • • • • • • •

There are also some things you can do before bringing up the subject with them. Find out as much as you can about being unemployed. It may be easier to talk to another adult outside the family first, like a teacher or a guidance counselor, or your priest, minister, or rabbi. Maybe one of your friends also has had a parent lose his or her job. You may get some comforting information from others who have experience with the situation.

It also helps to know some of the facts about being unemployed. Ask your librarian to guide you to some reading materials that explain how people cope with unemployment.

Try to remember that your father isn't the first person who's had to face losing his job.

Learning to Communicate

Once you've made up your mind to talk to your parents and have found out something about unemployment, there are ways to get over the hurdle of starting a conversation about the problem with them.

You may want to confide in a good friend and practice the conversation in advance.

■ Know what you want to achieve in your conversation. Do you really want to help your parents or do you just want to feel more secure about the future?

■ Plan in advance what you are going to say and how you will say it.

■ Decide when you are going to bring up the subject. It is best to talk at some quiet moment, when you are all relaxed and at ease. Be prepared to seize the moment when it appears; you may not know exactly when it will happen.

Opening the Conversation

Once you've started, the hardest part is over. You've already planned what you will say. You'll be able to say something like, "Dad, ever since you lost your job, I feel scared. I know things are rough for you and Mom now, but I need to talk to you both about what's going on."

Let them know that you are upset and understand how upset they must be. Tell them you want to share their problems and help work them out. Understand that your parents may not be able to respond instantly to you. They may be so frustrated and worried themselves, so unused to talking over problems of this kind with their children, that they cannot immediately pick up the conversation with you. You may have to wait a bit, or try another time, until they have grown used to the idea. It's even possible that they simply cannot talk with you and that you will have to wait until your father finds another job for family life to resume its normal course.

Most parents, however, will be grateful for the chance finally to explain the situation to their children and happy to have their cooperation.

Once family members talk openly about what a parent's unemployment means to the whole family, you can begin to pull together and share the burden. After the family begins to

Talking openly to your parents about unemployment is probably the best way to show them that you care and that you're willing to help out as much as you can.

Maybe you've always helped with the household chores. Your continued help during this stressful time will be especially appreciated.

communicate about this important issue, you'll find that there are many things you can do to help out—from taking on household chores to addressing envelopes to possible employers for your parents.

CHAPTER 2

Learning About Unemployment

Q My mother was laid off from her job. She's really upset and that scares me. Was she fired, or is "laid off" something different? I'm really confused. Can you help me understand what's going on?

A It is frightening to see your mother upset, especially if you don't know what has happened to her. Let's try to clear up your confusion. There is a difference between being laid off and being fired. Workers are fired because their work is poor or they acted improperly. Reasons for firing include an employee's inability to do the job, dishonesty, frequent absenteeism, or a violation of safety rules. In periods of slow business, a company may let a number of workers go in order to reduce costs. That is what has happened to your mother. This reduction in staff is called a layoff and has nothing to do with job performance. Layoffs are usually temporary, but they can last a long time.

How a person loses a job affects how much money and other benefits he or she can collect later on. Knowing as much as possible about unemployment will help you understand what happened to your mother. It will also prepare you to deal with job loss if it comes up again in your life or the lives of people around you.

• • • • • • • • • • •

We get many calls from teens who are worried about a parent losing a job. It can be a scary event—one that brings about major changes. If your parent has lost a job, or if you're worried about that happening, you'll feel better if you have some facts about unemployment. Here we'll tell you why people lose their jobs, explain the different ways employment can end, and talk about the help your parent might receive after losing his or her job.

Why People Lose Their Jobs

Why do people sometimes lose their jobs? These are some of the common reasons:

■ Change in the company (or agency, for public service workers). If a company is reorganized, managers may decide to reduce the number of employees. Sometimes entire departments are closed. When two companies merge, they may not need all the employees. Some workers may be invited to change to jobs that aren't being eliminated. People who decide not to change usually lose their jobs.

■ Loss of business. If a company's product or services aren't selling well, they may not be able to keep all of their workers. They may have to let go part of the staff permanently. Or they may call for a shutdown, or layoff, in which workers lose their jobs temporarily.

■ Company relocation. If a company moves to a place where business is better or costs are lower, employees may be invited to move with the company. Those who don't get invited, or who decide not to move, usually lose their jobs.

■ Retirement. People retire when they don't intend to work anymore. We don't usually think of retired people as unemployed. However, a company may invite people to take "early retirement." The employee agrees to leave earlier than planned and, in return, receives certain retirement benefits.

■ Resignation. People quit, or resign from, jobs when they decide to leave voluntarily. A person might do this for such reasons as illness, a change in the job, in order to care for a family member, a different job, or a disagreement about something at work.

■ Fired for cause. A person can get fired for failing to perform a job properly or for misconduct on the job.

Companies and their employees are affected by changes such as increased competition and the need to keep up with new technology. Some economic changes are strong enough to affect the entire nation, and some technological changes are strong enough to affect an entire industry.

Role of the Economy

Your parent and his or her former employer are part of a bigger picture—the national economy. The economy and the recession were big issues in the 1992 presidential election campaign. You may have heard a lot of talk about the economy but weren't quite sure what was being discussed. Here are a few simple facts to help you understand the big economic picture.

A recession is an economic slowdown. During a recession, people buy fewer goods and services, and businesses cut back on the number of goods and services they make or provide. Reduced production generally results in worker layoffs. A recession usually lasts for less than a year, and then the economy begins to recover. But if a recession lasts for a very long time and becomes more severe—as it did in the 1930s—it is called a depression.

Unemployment Rate by State

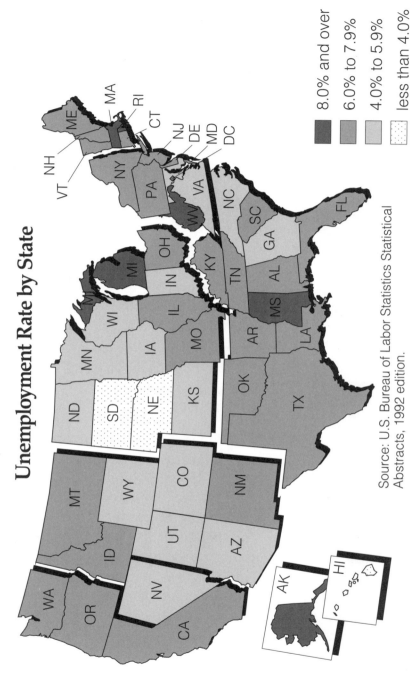

8.0% and over

6.0% to 7.9%

4.0% to 5.9%

less than 4.0%

Source: U.S. Bureau of Labor Statistics Statistical Abstracts, 1992 edition.

The United States experienced a significant decline in employment in the early 1990s. Hardest hit were manufacturing and agricultural regions.

When Tiffany's father was laid off from his job, her life changed. Tiffany tells what happened. "My dad was laid off with no warning. His boss told him, then boom, one week later Dad was jobless. I realize now that was unfair of me, but my feelings for my dad began to change. I had always really looked up to him, and now I felt ashamed of him. I lied to my friends and made up stories about why my dad wasn't at work. I was too embarrassed to tell them the truth. But I bet they knew I was lying all the time. Later I found out that some of their moms and dads had lost their jobs, too. Then I started getting a little wild, breaking curfew, not listening to my parents. I figured if he couldn't be a good dad and earn a decent living to support us, then I didn't have to listen to him. I thought I was being real tough and grown up, but I see now I was just running scared."

Tiffany had trouble concentrating on her schoolwork, and her grades began to fall. "I started skipping school. I got away with it for a while, then it caught up with me, and I got hauled into the guidance counselor's office. I had a real attitude about it and wouldn't talk to her. But Mrs. Mosley, the guidance counselor, wouldn't give up. She was so kind and understanding, I surprised myself . . . I sort of broke down. I started crying right there in her office. I was totally humiliated, but she was really cool about it. She whipped out a tissue and told me I wasn't the first kid to cry in her office. I calmed down and started talking. Mrs. Mosley helped me understand that it wasn't my dad's fault that he was unemployed and also that it didn't mean he would be unemployed forever. We talked about lots of stuff, and I realized that I had been acting up because I was scared. I had never talked to a guidance counselor before, and I ended up being real glad she made me talk. And I can always go see her if things get bad."

Tiffany's story emphasizes the need to understand what has happened and how you feel about it. By doing so, you can make things easier for yourself and your family.

Changing Technology

Technological advances have eliminated thousands of jobs in dozens of industries. Take the computer industry, for example. A few years ago, it took three chips to make a computer processor. Now, it takes only one. The people who made the other two chips are no longer needed. Similarly, when communications companies replaced copper wire with fiber optics, thousands of jobs were lost. Fiber optics enabled specialists to diagnose and resolve problems long-distance, thus eliminating the need for on-site repair crews. Although technological advances have eliminated some jobs, many new jobs have been created.

We've looked at some of the factors that may have contributed to your parent's job loss. Now let's consider what to do about it.

Timing: When a Parent Loses a Job

The amount of advance warning they have can make a big difference to people losing their jobs. Sometimes people are told beforehand about a company move or reorganization. This allows time for them to find out whether there's some way for them to stay on. If not, they have time to look for another job before this one comes to an end. The company may help employees to examine their options. It's a good idea to take advantage of every source of help offered by the company.

In other cases, workers may have little or no warning about a layoff or firing. Federal law requires companies that lay off a large number of workers to give at least two months' notice of the cutback. In small companies, the decision is entirely up to the employer.

Unemployment—with or without warning—is bad news. But there are things your family can do right away.

One of the first is to look into what benefits are available.

Unemployment Compensation and Other Benefits

In addition to a salary, there are other benefits connected with a job—paid vacation time, pensions, medical insurance, or a company car. Of course, most of these benefits stop when a worker is laid off. But you may be surprised to learn that some can continue. There also may be special assistance—provided by the employer or the government—for unemployed people.

■ Severance pay. Some employers will pay a sum of money, known as severance pay, to an employee who has been dismissed. This payment is in addition to regular wages. The amount may be based on the length of time spent working for the company, or the salary received, or both. If your parent received any severance pay, it can be used to meet the family's living expenses during his or her search for a new job.

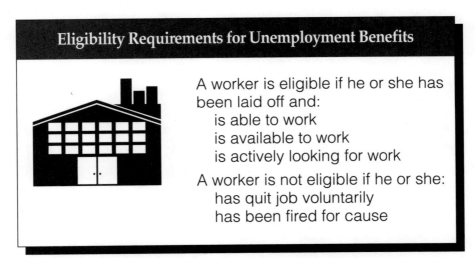

Eligibility Requirements for Unemployment Benefits

A worker is eligible if he or she has been laid off and:
    is able to work
    is available to work
    is actively looking for work

A worker is not eligible if he or she:
    has quit job voluntarily
    has been fired for cause

As unemployment reached record highs in the early 1990s, some unions negotiated for additional benefits to supplement the income unemployed workers received from state programs.

■ Unemployment compensation. Unemployment compensation is a state-run program that provides payments to people who lose their jobs through no fault of their own—as in the case of layoffs. These payments were established by the Federal Unemployment Insurance Act in the 1930s. This act set up minimum standards for unemployment benefits. Each state has the power to set its own policy, as long as the minimums are met. When unemployment is severe, the federal government may decide to extend the benefits. In 1991, for instance, Congress voted to extend unemployment benefits beyond the 26-week limit.

In order to receive unemployment compensation, a person has to be able to work, be available for work, and be actively looking for work. Not everyone is entitled to unemployment compensation. People who quit their jobs or who were fired for cause may not be eligible.

The best place to find out about unemployment benefits and how to apply for them is the state unemployment office. If your parent is eligible, he or she will receive a weekly check from this program. Unfortunately, the amount your parent receives will be less than what he or she was earning on the job. Still, it's better than no income at all.

Alaina learned about unemployment compensation through real life experience. She said, "My mother lost her job last year. Right away I knew we were in for trouble because she supports us all by herself. My dad lives in another state, and I don't see him much. He is supposed to pay child support, but Mom almost never gets any money from him, so she basically supports my brothers and me. Mom told us we'd have to cut back. She worked out a budget for us to follow, and it was drastic. Then I noticed that she was getting unemployment checks. I asked her what the problem was, since she was getting money from unemployment. I just figured she was being hyper about the unemployment thing. Mom got out the budget

In the early 1990s, unemployment rates in several major U.S. cities rose to more than ten percent. The number of people applying for unemployment benefits reached a 40-year high in 1991.

again and showed me all our expenses. Many of them, like rent and stuff, were the same as when she was bringing home a paycheck. Then she showed me the unemployment check. Boy, was I surprised when I saw how much less money it was than her paycheck had been! I guess I had the idea that unemployment compensation sort of just replaced your salary."

The discussion with her mother helped Alaina to see what was really going on with the family finances. She recalled, "I guess I grew up a little when my mom and I had that talk. I understood more what she was going through, and it was a lot easier for me to stick to our budget. I didn't feel like it was punishment any more. And I think it was easier to cut Mom some slack when she got tense, because I understood what she was going through."

Medical Benefits

Many jobs include health insurance coverage as an employee's benefit. Usually an employer or a trade union arranges for a health insurance company to pay for some or all of the medical care that workers and their families receive for illness or injury. The employer (or the union) and the workers contribute to the cost of the insurance. When someone leaves a job, it may be possible for the unemployed worker to remain on the company's health plan for a while. Although the worker may have to pay an additional cost to keep on the group plan, it will still be less expensive than an individual health plan. And having health insurance will be one less problem to worry about during this stressful time.

Some Important Issues to Remember

Learning that your parent lost his or her job has been a big shock for you, but it can be worse if you don't have enough information. What we've been discussing should help you to sort out what's happening. Here are a few more points to bear in mind:

■ Don't be tempted to blame anyone in particular, without knowing all the facts. It's natural for you to feel angry, but when someone loses a job, it's very often not that person's fault. It may not even be the fault of the supervisor or the head of the company. If the job had to be eliminated for business reasons, there may be no one to blame at all.

■ Remember that losing this job does not predict what will happen to your parent in his or her next job. Think over the reasons for losing jobs we've mentioned. The problem in the last job may have had something to do with that particular company or department. Even if your parent quit or was fired in a dispute with someone, things can improve.

■ During a recession, unemployment is unusually high, but even in normal times people lose their jobs or change them.

■ Remember that there are programs available to help your family through this difficult time. Severance pay and unemployment compensation may not equal your parent's former salary, but having this assistance could mean that there will be no need to panic.

■ You might also want to ask your parent if anyone else was dismissed. Knowing that your parent was not singled out could make an important difference in the way you both feel about the job loss.

CHAPTER 3

Effect on the Family

Q Ever since my dad lost his job, my parents have been so worried. They spend hours arguing about it. It's hard to be around them when they are like this . . . and they are like this more and more. What should I do?

A You are probably feeling confused. You are probably also feeling angry, sad, frustrated, and much more. All these feelings are normal. Your father's unemployment is affecting his relationship with your mother and the rest of the family as well. The loss of income may not be his only problem. Sometimes losing a job results in a whole series of personal problems for the unemployed person that affect the family, too. Your father is probably also feeling angry and frustrated. These feelings can make him lose his temper with your mother and other family members. Or it can make him feel depressed and isolated from the family. It is important for you to remember that this is his problem; you can't solve it. However, you can help by being patient and understanding when your dad just doesn't seem himself.

• • • • • • • • • • • •

Losing all or part of the family income can trigger a wide range of family problems. But there are things that you and your family can do to ease the strain. As you read this chapter, note the suggestions that you think will work best for your special situation.

Unemployment and Feelings About Self

When a parent loses a job, he or she loses more than money. People in our society often see themselves in terms of their jobs and by the things they can buy with their income. Many people base their self-worth on how much money they earn. Adults may compare their salaries to those of coworkers, friends, or neighbors. Television constantly bombards us with images of lavish lifestyles, and sometimes it's difficult to disting-

Even a modest neighborhood indicates a certain lifestyle that may be difficult to maintain after the loss of a job.

uish between real life and TV life. We also tend to judge ourselves by the status symbols our money can buy. Look at how television commercials encourage us to "move up to" a particular luxury car. Do you buy designer jeans or a particular brand of athletic shoes because they fit better or because they improve your image? Too often, we form our self-image by things—the neighborhood we live in, the clothes we wear, the car we drive. Little wonder, then, that when a parent loses a job, he or she probably feels a loss of self-worth as well.

Many people define themselves by what they are, not who they are. Adults meeting for the first time will usually be discussing their jobs within the first five minutes of conversation. A typical conversation might begin like this:

"Hello, I'm Bill Witherspoon."

"Hi, I'm Mary Flynn; pleased to meet you."

"Do you live in the city?"

"Yes, on the west side, and you?"

"Downtown. How do you know the McVeighs?"
"I work with Charlie at Davis and McCann."
"Oh, what do you do there?"

And the answer is something like: I'm the marketing director, I'm an administrative assistant, I'm a teacher, I'm an autoworker. So what happens when marketing directors or autoworkers find themselves unemployed? Suddenly they feel as if their identity has been stolen.

It may be easier for you to understand your parent's unusual and unpredictable behavior if you understand the ways in which unemployment is slowly destroying his or her sense of self-worth. Here are some of the signs you might observe in your parent. Seeing some or all of these may mean that your parent is depressed and is experiencing a problem with self-image:

■ Negative change in appearance—not dressing as neatly as usual, not shaving, not combing his or her hair.

■ Change in social life—avoiding friends, relatives, neighbors.

■ Change in sleeping habits—sleeping much longer than usual, sleeping much less than usual.

■ Irritability—quick loss of temper for seemingly small things.

■ Change in eating habits—not eating nearly enough, or eating too much.

If your unemployed parent is behaving in any of these ways, there may be a serious problem. Although this is your parent's problem, it is affecting you in a major way. You can first try talking to both parents about what is happening and its effect on you. But if your parent's problem persists, he or she might need some professional help.

The unemployment of a parent is upsetting to all members of the family. It helps both you and your parent to talk about how the situation affects the family, what changes may need to be made, and what you can do to help.

Your Self-Image: Changes in You

Your own sense of self-worth may have been affected by your parent's job loss. Maybe you now feel embarrassed when people ask what work your father or mother does. Or you may feel a loss of self-esteem because your family has less money to spend. Maybe you wonder if your friends will continue to accept you if you can't afford to buy the latest fashions, or if your spending money isn't comparable to theirs anymore.

If this sounds familiar, read Doug's story: "When my father lost his job," Doug recalled, "my whole world changed. I was really proud of my dad and his work. He is a construction worker and worked on a lot of the important buildings around here—the new high school, the hospital. I know we weren't rich, but we always seemed to have enough money for the basics, and my dad seemed to find ways of getting me the things I wanted. Like when I turned 16 and he bought this used car and fixed it up for me.

"Then he lost his job, and things were suddenly so different. Now I didn't know what to say when kids asked me what he did. It didn't seem like he was a construction worker anymore. It didn't seem like he was my dad anymore. He sat around the house all day. I didn't want to bring my friends home anymore because I felt so embarrassed. I mean there he was in the middle of the day, watching TV or just snoring away."

Doug told how the situation changed: "Things were pretty bad. We could all see Dad was depressed, but he didn't seem to want to do anything to change it. Mom—she's a nurse—she started working extra shifts to pay the bills. You would think that Dad would have been happy to see more money, but he got mad at her instead. He complained that she wasn't keeping the house clean like she used to. It just kept going from bad to worse for months. Then one of Dad's buddies called him about a job.

"I thought our problems were solved. But Dad said that he wouldn't take the job because it didn't pay as much as his last one. Mom said that he'd better take the job no matter what it paid. She also said that he'd gotten lazy and if he didn't take this job, or find another one, she was kicking him out. I couldn't believe what was happening. But maybe my dad had to hit rock bottom before he could get back up again.

"I felt like I had hit rock bottom, too. I didn't realize how much I was acting like my dad. I had let my schoolwork go. I was avoiding my friends—there was . . . like . . . nothing good in my life."

Doug's father took the job, but Doug said that his parents are in counseling to help heal the wounds caused by all the anger of the last few months. Doug also feels the scars. He's had some long talks with his school counselor, who is helping him regain his self-esteem.

Straining the Bonds of Marriage

Doug's story shows how parental unemployment can affect self-image. It also shows how it may affect your parents' marriage. Exactly how unemployment can affect a marriage depends, of course, upon the two people involved. But one thing is sure—unemployment will strain the relationship in some way. Because unemployment changes how people view themselves, it also changes how they act with others.

Sometimes when unemployment occurs, married couples argue about things that weren't problems before. Here are some examples from Hot Line callers:

■ Julie's dad used to help her mom with the dishes. But since he lost his job, he doesn't want to help with the housework anymore. He yells at Julie's mom that just because he is home all day, it doesn't mean he's a housewife.

■ Jody's father complains when his wife tries to do something nice for him. He accuses her of "babying" him.

■ Freddie's mom doesn't care about her appearance since she lost her job. She looks kind of sloppy. When Freddie's father tries to encourage his wife to "fix herself up," she cries that he doesn't love her anymore.

A job loss can often strain a marriage and lead to discussions between husband and wife that can be disturbing for children.

All these parents are experiencing changes in their relationships. When something stressful, like unemployment, happens, it is a common response to lash out at those close to us. It is not a good thing to do, but it is a very human response to a painful situation.

Changes in Your World

As we've seen, unemployment affects everyone in the family. Your parents may respond to the situation in a variety of ways. They may try to shelter you from the bad news, which makes you feel like a small child. On the other hand, they might be feeling overwhelmed. You may feel that they're asking too much of you, leaving you little time for homework and friends.

Your parent may have become distant from you. Perhaps your parent feels that by being unemployed, he or she has failed you as a parent. Generally, if a parent's behavior has changed since the job loss, it's due to that and is probably temporary. But until your parent gets a new job, you will need some coping strategies to help you through this rough period.

Understanding Your Parent
Take a minute right now to think about what your parent is going through. This may make it easier for you to react in a more sensitive way the next time your mom or dad is a little stressed out and treats you in a manner that you feel you don't deserve.

Take Time Out for You
Maybe you are a teen who really pitches in and helps the family. If so, you are probably already doing a lot during this family crisis. Be sure that you take time out for you. If you've stopped spending time with your friends, or if you are doing so much at home that your grades are slipping—these are signs that you need to take more time for yourself and your needs.

Get Some Tension Relief

If you're feeling especially tense when you're at home, find some relief. Do you enjoy running, swimming, or other exercise? Now is a particularly good time to start a regular exercise program. Experts say that regular exercise is one of the best ways to eliminate stress. So, maybe you don't like exercise. What about a hot bath? A heart-to-heart talk with your best friend? Be creative, and you'll think of some more fun things to help get you through.

Get Extra Help

You may find that things at your house are so bad that none of these suggestions will work for you. Have you stopped caring about your friends? Are you paying less attention to your schoolwork? Are your parents so involved in their own problems that they haven't noticed yours? Does your life feel out of control? If any of this describes you, get some help now.

Your school has a guidance counselor, a school social worker, or a school psychologist. Don't be afraid to tell one of these people what is happening. Whatever you say to a school counselor is confidential and will be kept private. School counselors are specially trained to help you. And don't be surprised if you get very emotional, or even cry when you talk to them. You have lots of feelings that you've been keeping inside. We'd be surprised if you don't feel relieved after you share the burden by talking. Your school counselor can help you develop the coping strategies you need during your parent's unemployment.

In addition, your other parent or an older sister or brother may have access to an Employee Assistance Program (EAP) at work. If so, you and every member of your family are entitled to three or four hours of free counseling. Check it out!

CHAPTER 4

Finances

Q First Dad loses his job. Then I heard we weren't going to the beach this summer. Now my mom tells me my allowance is being cut in half! What's the deal here? I think they ought to be able to handle this better, without cutting out all the fun in life. What do you think?

A It does sound like your family is cutting expenses in a serious way. It's quite natural that you feel angry, and down deep, you're probably worried, too. If possible, you should go to your parents and tell them how you feel about the situation. Talking things through with them is the best way to understand what's happening and to help clear up any bad feelings in the family.

• • • • • • • • • • • •

There also may be another way for your family to handle the financial crunch they're in now. You can be a part of it.

Analyzing Expenses

In order to cope with changes that unemployment is causing in your family, it can help to do a "family financial analysis." Get your family to sit down together. Ask your parents if they would be willing to discuss their income and expenses. They may object to giving you exact figures. But they probably won't mind discussing expenses in a general way. It should be possible to divide expenses into those that are absolutely necessary and those that are not. Every family's financial situation is unique, but the necessary expenses in many families commonly include food, rent or mortgage payments, clothing, insurance (medical, life, disability, household, and car), taxes, telephone, heating, gas or other transportation expense, and interest payments.

That's quite a list. It may be that you have not been aware of where the money goes in your family. Learning about your family's financial picture can be a real eye-opener for a lot of kids. Even if there is a severe financial problem, knowing just where things stand can take some of the mystery and fear away. It may even help you to be a part of solving the family's financial burden.

Setting Priorities

Now that you've learned about the necessary family expenses, make a list of ordinary family expenses on extras, such as entertainment (movies, video rentals, CDs), eating out, haircuts and manicures, extra clothes, music lessons, Boy Scouts, charitable contributions, or memberships in the Y. With this list plus the necessary expenses list in hand, see if you can't set spending priorities as a family. For example, spending money on gas to drive to a job interview is a high priority. Spending money on gas to cruise with your friends, while fun, is not essential.

Each family will make different choices. If all family members decide together what to cut from the budget, all will feel like they're sharing the burden.

Reducing Expenses

Erika's family attacked the issue of reducing expenses in a creative way. "When my dad lost his job, I was really scared. Then Dad said that we would face this as a family. He and Mom

Mom talked about ways we could all help. We even made a joke that we were part of a new minority, the `financially challenged,' and it felt good to laugh again. As we talked things out, I began to realize that since my dad lost his job, we'd all been living in stress city.

"We decided to see who could cut the most `fat' out of our budget. I started making my own lunch instead of buying it at the school cafeteria." Erika laughed as she recalled, "Between the greasy cafeteria fries I was missing and walking to school instead of driving, I had the added bonus of losing three pounds that I needed to drop."

Erika and her family found ways to cut down on extras. They were able to reduce their cash outflow quite a bit without drastically changing their style of living. And once they started thinking about ways to slash their unnecessary spending, it became a good habit.

Keeping Accounts

After cutting expenses has become a family priority, it is all the more important to keep track of what the family spends. Your parents will take care of the major part of this. You can help by keeping a record of your personal expenses.

Keeping your own accounts is the best way to set priorities for your spending. Buy a small notebook and faithfully write down in it every penny you spend. Or, if it works better, have your parents open a checking account for you. You will have to keep a careful record of your spending in order to balance your checkbook. You may be surprised at the amount you spend, and have to cut back even more. At least you will be in control of your money and doing your part to help the family. And the lessons you learn in money management now will serve you the rest of your life.

Zak, age 14, had to deal with slashing spending and setting priorities when his mother lost her job. Zak remembered,

"Living with a single mom, I thought I was already used to scrimping and saving. I helped with the cooking at home and did a lot of chores around the house. I didn't have a very big allowance, and it had to cover lunches, school dances, snacks, magazines, tapes, and movies. But I was blown away when I started a daily expense ledger. By the end of the first month, I realized that I spent a lot on soda and gum. I bought sports magazines, when I could read them in the library. Once I started seeing where all the money went, I got better control over managing it. I made a list of the stuff I really wanted and the stuff I could do without, and I kept careful track in my ledger of what I bought. Soon I found I wasn't begging my mom for extra money, which used to make her mad. And after a while, I found I wasn't even missing the stuff I didn't buy. Besides, I had saved almost enough to buy a new Cubs hat!"

Increasing Resources

When unemployment happens, most people think of cutting expenses. This is critical, but families should also think of looking for other ways to increase their incomes. Every family has hidden resources. Resources may include items to sell, talents to put to work, or new ideas to save money. Think hard about your family and all the resources it has at its disposal.

Why not hold a family meeting and brainstorm ideas together? It's a great way to find some solutions to problems. To brainstorm with your family, have every family member speak in turn about his or her ideas. Don't interrupt or criticize. When you've all had a chance to speak, talk about each idea to find the ones that work best for your family.

Here are a few suggestions that might stimulate your family's discussion:

■ Can the family find ways to buy food and prepare healthful meals more economically?

A garage sale or tag sale is a good way to get rid of the items your family doesn't use anymore—and make some money at the same time.

■ Can the family clean out the attic and the garage and hold a garage sale?

■ If your family has a garden, could you plant vegetables as well as flowers?

■ Is there a possibility of carpooling with neighbors to save on gas money?

■ Can you expand your own family chores (dog walking, lawn mowing) into services for your neighbors to earn extra money? Could you save your parents baby-sitting money by caring for younger brothers or sisters? Be creative. Turn a tough situation into a positive search for family resources that can provide extra income or savings and some fun for everybody.

Community Resources

Your community may have resources to offer your family as well. For example, your church may sponsor a swap meet where you can trade your old microwave oven for some garden tools you need. Or your church or library may have a job referral service. Another community organization, like the YMCA or the local adult school, might have courses for your parents to update job skills, like computer training. A local group might sponsor a food co-op that purchases foods in bulk. If your family joins the co-op, you can usually buy food at prices lower than at the supermarket.

Community resources vary widely. A small rural town will offer very different opportunities from those found in a large city. Ask your local librarian to help you begin to research your community's resources. You may be really surprised at what you will find.

State or federal economic assistance—such as Aid to Families with Dependent Children and food stamps—may be available for families with severe problems. Information is available at your county Board of Social Services.

To Work or Not to Work?

Many teenagers ask whether they should look for a job when a parent is out of work. There is no simple answer to this question. You may want to get a job to help with family finances. Your parents may need to ask you to get a job to contribute to the family income. It is essential for you to discuss this with your parents.

No matter why you are considering working, your parents may worry that your schoolwork will suffer as a result of your having a job. It may be reassuring for your parents to know that studies have shown that teens with jobs do as well or better than teens without jobs! Experts say that teens with jobs tend to be better organized and more disciplined with the free time that they do have. A good rule of thumb is that working ten hours a week or less tends not to interfere with school or homework. You must balance all the pros and cons that taking a job would create in your situation. First, of course, you should find out as a teen whether you'll need working papers and at what age. Talk to your school counselor about this.

■ Should you contribute to the family income? A job may supply necessary cash for the family or cover your own extra expenses. An alternative might be to take on extra household tasks that will free a parent to work longer hours. You should discuss this thoroughly with your parents.

■ What if a job meant you had to give up the football team? It isn't easy to give up a favorite sport or other activity at which you excel. So you must feel that it is important for you to do so. You and your parents must discuss your feelings about this. A job well done can bring many satisfactions for you—just like

You may be thinking about getting a job to help with the family's expenses. If so, be sure that the job will not interfere with your current obligations, such as schoolwork.

football. However, a job requires the same kind of commitment that you give to your football team. You must be reliable and perform your best. Otherwise you won't keep your job. Only you can decide if you are ready to take on the new responsibility.

■ What if your grades start slipping after you get a job, but you desperately need the money? Don't panic. It may be that you have not yet learned to organize your time. See your guidance counselor as soon as possible. You may be able to find ways to get everything done without sacrificing either your grades or your job.

Getting your first job helps you take an important step toward adult independence, but it can create many pressures. Talk about your concerns with your parents and a school guidance counselor in order to make the right choice for yourself.

What About College?

Getting into college is a matter of great concern for many teenagers from the moment they enter high school. It's true that college costs are rising every year, and your parent's unemployment is certainly a worry. However, parental income is considered in financial aid applications. As a result, reduced income may actually make you eligible for aid you wouldn't have previously qualified for.

You can also get financial help through scholarships.

Even though a parent is out of work and tuition may be out of the question, many colleges offer aid to students in need of funds to go on with their education.

Even if you are not a candidate for an academic or athletic scholarship, you may qualify for scholarships you are presently unaware of. Check with the colleges of your choice and your guidance counselor to find out about any specific scholarships you might qualify for. You may find a scholarship that is tailor-made for you—one for a Native American who wants to major in art, for example, or one for females of Norwegian descent. Also check scholarships offered by religious, community, alumni, or business groups. Financial aid experts say that there is usually less competition for these little-known scholarships.

Finally, most state colleges provide good educations at very low cost. You might consider living at home, working part time, and attending college part time until your family's crisis has passed. You may then be able to move to full-time status. Or you might consider going to a two-year college now, and enrolling in a four-year college or university to complete your education later.

Yes, when a parent loses a job, the family has to make do with less money. It can be hard, and you may be asked to make sacrifices that are difficult. But cutting back on spending isn't impossible, and you can find ways to earn money to help out the family. Life may be tough for a while, but working together can help bring your family closer together. Remember, too, that whatever you learn about managing money now should help you later in life.

Interview

Shana was 16 when her father's unemployment made it necessary for the family to move. She found the thought of leaving the place where she (and her parents before her) had grown up both horrifying and depressing. Then a new friend showed Shana the positive side of the move.

My name is Shana. My father lost his job last July; he was a carpenter. He had worked for this same company forever. I never really thought about unemployment too much before it hit. It was just some kind of blah-blah that you hear on the news. Dad is a good carpenter, so when he told me about his job, I just told him to cheer up, that he'd get a new job. He explained that it wasn't going to be that easy . . . . He said that there wasn't too much building going on anywhere in the country, but that our city was real bad.

It sort of took a while for things to sink in. I guess I just thought things would get better somehow. Dad went out looking for work every day, but I have to say that I didn't pay too much attention. I was busy with my friends and my own life, and I didn't really pay too much attention to him. One day he told us that there was just no hope of him finding work here and that he had to begin to look for work somewhere else.

I was born here and so were my parents. All of my friends were from here, and I never really thought about living anywhere else. But when he started talking about looking for work far away, I fell out of my little safety net. It was like I woke up all of a sudden and realized that our lives were going to change in a major way.

Dad said that nothing was definite . . . not to panic. He said that he was just going to start looking, that we weren't going anywhere yet. But I had this sinking feeling in my stomach. I just knew that we would have to move, that I would have to move away from my school, from our apartment, from all my friends, from the rest of our family . . . from everything. I became really depressed. Mom and Dad tried to cheer me up and kept saying that nothing was definite, but I knew we were going to have to go. So when he finally told me that he had found a job in another state, I wasn't surprised at all.

I can't say I was ready, because it still hurt . . . it hurt so bad. I can still remember the pain in my stomach that day he said we were moving.

I tried to make the time I had left last as long as possible. I know that might sound a little crazy, but when Dad went on ahead to start his new job and Mom and I had two months to pack up our things and stuff, I just tried to make time last. I did stuff like try to stay up as late as I could every night, just to make each day last longer. I woke up early, too. I figured I could catch up later, after we moved. But I wanted to spend every minute I could with my friends. And even though I wouldn't have believed it, I started loving going to school, well not exactly loving it, but it was real different all of a sudden. I kept thinking every time I walked down the halls that pretty soon I wouldn't be able to walk down those halls.

Everything I did, even dumb things I took for granted . . . like going for a pizza after school with my friends, seemed so special.

I cried a lot . . . especially at night before I went to sleep. I didn't want to, and I felt dumb about it, but it seemed like the tears wouldn't stop.

Then the day finally came. It was the day that I had to say goodbye to everyone at school and all my friends. It was rotten. I took lots of pictures so that I would be able to remember people. My friends promised to write, and we gave each other gifts. They even threw a party for me at the pizza place. They had my name spelled out in peppers on the pizza. That was so dumb, but so nice. I totally embarrassed myself by crying in front of everyone. Then we were all hugging. And then it was all over, and my mother and I were driving to meet Dad.

When we got to our new town, Mom acted all excited, but I could tell she was pretty upset too. But as sad as it was, it was good to see Dad again. He had been living here since he got the new job, and we hadn't seen him for a couple of months. It felt good to be a family again, but that was the only good thing I can say about it.

I remember when I started at my new school. It was very hard. The math classes were totally different from the ones at my old school, so I had to go back a semester. That made me feel, like, really stupid. I felt like I didn't fit in well . . . in just about every way. The school was smaller than my old school, and it felt like a small town where everyone knew everyone else—except me. It was like I didn't exist. I kept thinking of all of my friends, going to our old places, doing all our favorite things.

I was pretty miserable for about three months. You would think my grades would have been fantastic, because I never hung out with friends; I just went right home after school. But I just sat around and watched TV and stuff. I spent lots of time writing long letters to my old friends about how terrible this place was.

I guess what finally started changing things for me was when I met Nina. She was another transfer student. She came about a month after me. I thought, well, here's someone who's newer than me; she'll be even more miserable. But Nina seemed to fit in right away. She would just go up to groups of kids she didn't know, and start talking to them. I thought they'd tell her to take a hike, but she started making friends. I decided to make friends with her. She seemed so positive, and I was sick and tired of feeling sick and tired. When I started meeting new kids with Nina, things started to get a little better.

I still miss all my old friends, and I write to them all the time. But I got a grip on reality. I just told myself, you live here now, so get over it. And I have started. Nina is more friendly and outgoing than I am, so I kind of hang around with her, and that's really worked. I have made a couple of new friends, and they even have this crazy idea that I should join the pep squad at school, because they're on it. So I'm going to do that.

This is my new home now, so I guess I'm going to have to learn to live here . . . and enjoy it.

CHAPTER 5

Relocation

Q | I am in a panic! I live with my mother. She lost her job six months ago. After job hunting all this time—and still no job, she now says that desperate times call for desperate measures. She's looking for a cheaper apartment in our town and is also looking for jobs in other cities. What if we have to move to a new neighborhood, or worse, across the country? Is it really necessary to move? How will I survive it if we do?

A | Don't panic. Yes, your family's situation is serious, but your mother seems to be considering expanding her employment options, and that will benefit the whole family in the long run. When unemployment lasts longer than a few months, as your mother's has, it is appropriate to look farther afield. The two most common ways of doing so are looking outside one's usual area of employment and job hunting outside of one's local area. Your mother is feeling that after six months of job hunting in your community, she wants to enlarge her job search. At the same time she is exploring ways to decrease the family's expenses by looking for a cheaper apartment. The steps your mother is taking are sensible and should increase her chances of finding a job. Still, any move your family might need to make, whether across town, or across the country, will present problems—and challenges—for you.

• • • • • • • • • • •

Moving to a new place—even without the added hassles of a parent's unemployment—is a big deal. However, there are some strategies to make relocation less painful.

Families on the Move: You Are Not Alone

Years ago, most Americans spent their lives in one place surrounded by their extended families (their aunts, uncles, cousins, grandparents, and other relatives), in addition to their immediate, or nuclear, family (parents and children). The whole community was more unchanging and familiar. Today, experts agree that we are becoming an increasingly mobile society. If you and your family need to relocate, you join millions of Americans who move each year. And as these families are on the move, relocating to other communities, they are also becoming more isolated because they leave family and friends behind. One big reason for this is the changing job market which, in turn, has increased the need for many families to relocate.

Economic Reasons for Relocation

We all need money to exist in our society. When a parent's source of income ceases, he or she needs to find new employment. There are many national and international economic reasons for high unemployment in the United States right now. Decreased consumer spending, for example, has created less demand for products and services. To reduce operating expenses, employers may lay off a large number of workers. Or the entire company may go out of business, relocate to another state, or even move to another country. You may have heard about this during the recent presidential campaign when some American companies were criticized for relocating manufacturing plants to other countries with a cheaper available labor force, like Mexico, for example.

Moving to a new place doesn't have to be painful. The more you can learn in advance about your new town, the easier the transition will be.

Furthermore, as the work environment becomes increasingly automated, computers and machines have replaced human workers in many job situations. Workers who are laid off must look for jobs elsewhere.

Relocating for a New Job

According to the U.S. Census, the average American moves 12 times in a lifetime. The move you make now is only one of many you may have to make during your life. There may be no job for your parent in your current location, or perhaps your parent feels that he or she needs to relocate in order to make a career advance. Or you may be living in an area of the country that is economically depressed, and your parent may feel the need to move to another area where the local economy is better.

Temporary Moves
Sometimes relocation is only temporary. Perhaps your parent's company has a temporary assignment for him or her in another location. Or perhaps a department of a company, or even the entire company, is relocating to another part of the country, and your parent chooses to relocate temporarily until he or she can find another job back in your old community. There are many practical reasons why your family may need to relocate temporarily.

Kristin's story illustrates what you might encounter. Kristin said, "When my dad got a job offer, the whole family was thrilled. Dad was relieved because he'd been laid off from his old job for more than two months and he was getting pretty depressed. He would sit in front of the tube every night drinking beer after beer. It wasn't like him at all. He and Mom had lots of arguments about money, and it was horrible to be around them. Then his company found this temporary opening for him. Trouble was, this job was 350 miles away, and we had to move. I was miserable from the beginning. I tried to be happy that Dad had a job, any job. But it seemed like all the changes were bad ones. The town where Dad's new job was located was more expensive to live in than our old town, so we had to move into a much smaller apartment. I went from having my own small, but peaceful, bedroom to sharing a room with my two younger bratty sisters. Not pleasant, I can tell you. Mom said it wasn't so bad, because it was only temporary; Dad's company was going to let him transfer back to a job in our old town as soon as `something opened up.' But who knew how long that would be . . . my whole life probably, I thought. And Mom and Dad were so happy about the job, they didn't seem to notice that my whole life was ruined."

Kristin told how she eventually adjusted, "At first, things were terrible when we moved. The kids at my new school came from families with money. They had better clothes, more spending money. I felt like I was from another planet. But then I started to make friends. I had this weird feeling that nobody would want to be my friend because we were only living there temporarily and because we weren't rich. But then I realized I probably wasn't sending out the best vibes, so I made an attitude adjustment and tried hard to make new friends. I found out that not everybody at my new school was a snob. I eventually made some new friends. It wasn't like being part of my old group back home, but I did kind of drag myself out of the sea-of-loneliness feeling I lived in after we first moved. The move was really hard. I was in heaven when we finally got to move back to our old town about a year and a half later. But I guess it all had been worth it to see Dad back on his feet. He stopped drinking and didn't fight with Mom anymore."

Commuting Parents
Sometimes a parent will commute a distance to a job so that the whole family doesn't have to be uprooted. This may mean that your parent may work in another city during the week and commute home to the family on weekends, for example.

This was the case for the father of 16-year-old Teruko, who recalled, "When my father lost his job, he looked for work all over town. After three months of looking hard, he decided to expand his search and look for jobs in some larger cities. Three months later, he had a job offer in another county. He didn't want to go that far away, but he had no other job offers. My sister and I stayed with my mom in our house. My dad shared an apartment with two other guys from his new job. Dad said the drive took too long and was too expensive anyway, so he could only come home once a month. My sister and I were scared that our parents were going to get a divorce. It seemed in a way like they were divorced—my dad's life was so separate from ours. It was a scary time, and I cried a lot at night in my room when no one could see me."

Often parents find commuting long distances to a job only a temporary solution. Either they find another job back in their home community, or they decide to stay at the new job and relocate the family to live with them. Teruko told how her family solved the problem. "After my father had worked at his new job for almost half a year, he and my mom told us that we were all going to move to join him. It felt like kind of a no-win situation, because if we had stayed at our old home, we never saw our dad. If we moved to join him, it meant leaving our house, our neighborhood, my school and friends. Moving was hard and it took a while to adjust to the move."

The Big Move

No matter why or how your family relocates, things will be difficult. Experts say that any major life change is stressful, even positive change. So even if your parent gets a better job, at a larger salary, and you move to a bigger house or a better neighborhood, relocation will still be difficult for you and your family. However, there are some steps you can take to make relocation easier for you.

The first step is to let yourself feel sad. You are not only leaving a major part of your life—your best friend, your favorite teacher, the soccer team—but the many small things that made up the fabric of your life. Maybe it is the tree you and your parents planted in the front yard when you were little or the burger joint where you went on your first date. Leaving your friends will probably be the hardest part. Friends are very important in your teen years. Whatever you will miss, don't fight your feelings. If you want to cry, or get angry, it's OK.

As a teen you are also seeking more control and responsibility in your life as you mature. And part of this maturation, or growing-up process, means that you are becoming increasingly independent. This makes your family's relocation perhaps more difficult for you than it would be for someone younger, because it's something you have no control over and may make you feel helpless. Acknowledge all these disturbing feelings that are raging within you and make up your mind that you have to deal with them.

The next step is to actually deal with all these emotions. Talking with your parents and friends is a good way to begin. They may have similar feelings about the move. You may even find some friends who have gone through a relocation and can tell you how they handled it. Your school guidance counselor is no doubt very familiar with this situation and may also have specific suggestions for you.

Photos of friends taken before you have to relocate will help both you and them to ease the strain of being separated.

Jaime was at the end of his junior year in high school when he had to relocate with his family. It was a very tough time as he recalled: "I was looking forward to being a senior, for . . . well, just about my whole life. I couldn't believe that I had to leave my school just as I was going to be a senior. I thought of everything I would miss—my girlfriend, the senior prom, my place on our school's winning basketball team. . . ." His face became serious, then sad as he remembered this painful time, "I can't even list all the things that I was losing . . . I was losing everything."

Jaime was so depressed that he and his family went for some family counseling. The counselor suggested some things that Jaime could do to deal with his feelings and to start taking control. Jaime remembered, "I kind of thought counseling was for weirdos, or losers, but it turned out to be sort of cool. The counselor told me some things I could do to feel better, and I have to admit she was right. She told me to say good-bye not only to my friends, but to all the people—and places—that were special in my life. Many of my friends promised to write and phone, and I felt like I wasn't losing touch with everyone forever.

"I took pictures of some of my friends at our favorite hangouts, as well as a secret meeting place we had as kids, and made copies so we could all have these pictures. I also made some plans to be a small part of senior year. I had my best friend promise to order the senior yearbook for me and get all my old friends to sign it. It still really tore me up to leave, but doing these things made it not as bad."

Jaime's story illustrates the third step—taking control. Counselors agree that taking control of the situation can help you feel better. You might not be able to help having to move, but you can control how you deal with it. Jaime deliberately said good-bye to people and places that were important in his life and took mementos away with him. Jaime had his yearbook and photos; you decide what's important for you. Confronting your emotions and dealing with them will help you gain control over the situation. You will feel less depressed when you realize that leaving people, places, and things doesn't have to mean losing them.

Easing the Transition
The other important part of the process is to deal with the move itself. The more preparation you can make in advance, the easier the move will be for you when it happens. First research your new town. How much can you find out about it? Check out its cultural activities, sports teams, climate. Also, if time and budget allow, can you visit the town or city before you move? Perhaps you can accompany your parents on a house- or apartment-hunting trip. Even better—if you can—visit the new school you'll be attending. If you see how the kids there dress and act (maybe go to a school activity, like a track meet), you'll know more about what to expect when you get there, and you'll feel more a part of things from the very beginning.

Even if your relocation only means a move to the other side of town, it will still probably be hard for you. You may have to go to a new school and will live in a new neighborhood. It will be easier though for you to scout out your new surroundings than for someone who has to move far away, so take advantage of that fact before the move.

And try using your friends to make connections in new places. For example, you may have a friend who knows someone who lives in your new neighborhood or goes to your new school. Ask your friend to write or call that person and tell him or her about you. Whether you are moving near or far, try to make the move as easy for yourself as possible.

A New Life: You're in the Driver's Seat

Just as taking control can help you before the move, it can help you afterward, as well. Here are some general suggestions that often help ease the discomfort of being in a new environment.

First, be friendly. It sounds simple, but it works. Don't wait for kids at your new school to approach you. You can take the first step. Take any opportunity that naturally presents itself to get acquainted. For example, you could compare notes with someone after history class. Or perhaps if you like someone's outfit, you could let that person know. People always appreciate honest compliments. Also, you could sign up for as many activities as you have time for. Sharing an interest is a great way to make new friends, whether it's the French Club, the volleyball team, or the school choir.

Second, be yourself. When starting a conversation or giving a compliment, be genuine. Don't be so desperate to make friends that you act unnaturally.

Third, be patient. It can be hard being the new kid on the block, but if you naturally continue to be open to new friendships, you'll eventually find people you'll enjoy.

And last, don't fall into the "insecure and obnoxious" trap. Don't turn others off by telling them how great everything was at your old school, or how popular you were with your old crowd. It's tempting to brag in this way if you're feeling lonely in your new environment, but there's no faster way to turn potential new friends away.

If you are facing a relocation, it's hard to believe that life can ever be good again—but it can, and it's possible that life can even be better. This is a great chance for your family to pull closer together. You are also on the verge of meeting all kinds of interesting new people and coming into contact with new places and things. If you take control of the situation and focus on what you can gain, instead of what you feel you've lost, you can make the most of your move. Learning how to deal with this move now can help prepare you for later moves you will likely have to make in life.

CHAPTER 6

The Job Search

 Q My name is Malik. My mom has been supporting our family since I was little. Now she's lost her job, and I'm worried she won't find a new one. How can I help her?

 A Your mother is lucky to have a son who is so concerned. There are four things you can consider, all of which may help your mother. First, help relieve your mother of some of the housework and family chores so she can concentrate on her job search. Maybe you can help prepare simple meals for you and your younger brothers and sisters, do the grocery shopping, or take the other kids out for a walk or to a park from time to time to give your mom some rest. You can also baby-sit when she's out for job interviews.

Second, remember to do things just for you. A great way to help your mom right now is to make sure she doesn't have to worry about you. Maintain your grades, keep seeing your friends, and participate fully in your regular school and outside activities. Knowing that you are carrying on despite the problems caused by her unemployment will make your mom feel good and allow her to focus her energy on her job search.

Next, keep the lines of communication open. Share your concerns with your mom. Also, let her know she can talk to you. Single parents have a lot of responsibility; knowing that you care helps your mom a lot.

And last, there are several ways that you can help your mother with the actual job-search process.

The Job-Search Process

When someone loses his or her job, it is important for that person to start looking for a new job as soon as possible. One of the most important elements in the job search, for most people, is the resumé.

Preparing a Resumé: An Employment Calling Card
A resumé is a brief listing of a person's job history and related accomplishments. A resumé is sent to a potential employer, for example, in response to a classified newspaper ad about a job opening. According to experts these are the dos and don'ts for resumés that are really effective:

■ *Do* list specific past job accomplishments as well as job duties and responsibilities.

■ *Do* be as brief as possible. A compact, one- or two-page resumé is best.

■ *Do* keep it professional looking. The resumé is representing your parent so neatness and accuracy count.

■ *Don't* print the resumé on anything but white or ivory-colored paper. A resumé on lavender paper may look colorful, but it will get the wrong kind of attention.

■ *Don't* list age, marital status, or graduation dates. The law prohibits discrimination on the basis of age or marital status, so this information isn't relevant.

A neat, informative resumé can help your parent get a new job. Ask your parent if there is some way you can help prepare the resumé. You can offer to type it or proofread it for errors. Let your parent know that you've been reading up on resumés and that you know how important they are.

Don't be disappointed if your parent doesn't want to share the resumé with you. He or she may consider it too private. However, if your parent responds to your offer openly and willingly, you may be able to make some suggestions that will improve the resumé. You can certainly make sure there are no typing errors. A resumé should be letter perfect.

Employment Counselors

Your parent may see an employment counselor to aid in the job search. Employment counselors deal with many companies that have jobs available. The employment agencies match available jobs with potential job applicants, like your parent.

Some employment agencies are run by state or local governments. Their help is free. Others are private businesses that charge a fee for finding potential employees. Usually the employer pays the fee, but it's a good idea to check on each agency's policy.

There are employment counselors for all kinds of jobs—secretarial and administrative jobs, professional and management jobs, manual labor jobs, and more. What job seekers should bear in mind is that an interview with an employment counselor is just as important as a job interview with a prospective employer. Your parent should be neat, well groomed, and prepared for such an interview. You can help by:

■ Offering to help get your parent's interview outfit ready. Maybe you can iron a shirt, polish shoes, or sew on a button.

■ Offering to have your parent's resumé copied so that he or she can attend the interview well-prepared with several copies of the resumé ready.

Employment counselors and employment agencies try to match available jobs with qualified applicants. An interview with an employment counselor is just as important as an interview with a prospective employer.

■ Telling your parent how great he or she looks when your mother or father is all dressed up and ready to leave the house for a job interview. That's a real confidence booster that will surely help right now. Sometimes it's the little things that count the most.

Networking: Friends Can Help Make Contacts

Networking means contacting friends and family to help in the job-search process. It's an effective technique for finding new jobs.

Friends, friends of friends, coworkers of friends, and rela-

Networking is an important way for your parent to renew old contacts and make new ones. Anyone your parent knows, or meets, can be a potential contact for a job.

tives . . . anyone your parent knows, however distantly, can be a potential contact for a job.

Andrea's mother used her networking skills when she lost her job. Andrea explained how networking works. "My mom found out that she would be laid off in two weeks. She came home the night she found out and just cried. But after a few days, she started getting it together. She decided to get some help from her company in the time she had left there. She went to the human resources department in her company and talked to a person she said was an employment specialist. She asked this lady to give her some tips on her resumé. The specialist told Mom some ways she could improve her resumé. Then she told Mom about networking and never to leave a meeting or conversation about a job without the name of a new person to contact.

"Mom went home and started using what she learned. Mom called her friend Sally and asked if they were hiring at Sally's workplace. Sally said no, so Mom asked Sally if she had any friends who worked where they might be hiring. Sally told Mom about another friend . . . who Mom then called. Mom started networking and got real creative about it. Eventually she found a job that she got through information—get this—from our apartment building's superintendent's wife's sister's husband's best friend. If she hadn't started networking, she might still be unemployed."

There are many people your parent could network with to help in the job search. Maybe you can sit down with your parent and help make a list of people he or she can contact to start the process.

More Ways to Help

There are other ways you can help your parent in the job search. Consider the suggestions listed below.

Phone Messages

If your family doesn't have a phone message center, create one. This doesn't need to be fancy, and you don't need to buy anything. Just make sure there are always pens or pencils and a pad to write messages on in a specified place near the phone. Then have the whole family agree on where messages will be left—on a bulletin board, stuck to the refrigerator with magnets, on a hall table. It doesn't matter where it is, as long as all phone messages are always left in that same place.

You can also help by willingly taking complete and accurate phone messages. Your parent could lose out on a potential job with a message like "Mom, Mr. Berger called," when your mother doesn't know who Mr. Berger is or what company he is calling from. Remember these important suggestions when you take any job-related phone message for your parent:

Ask the caller to spell his or her first and last name. Take down the phone number and read it back to the caller.

Ask what specific message you can give your parent; for example, is it urgent that your parent call back as soon as possible, or does the caller want your parent to come for a job interview and if so, when?

Write neatly. This sounds pretty obvious, but if your parent can't read the entire message, including return phone number, the message may be useless.

Local Resources

If your parent is having trouble with the job-seeking process, perhaps you could do some research to find out about local resources. Does your local unemployment office have any free seminars on resumé writing or job-seeking skills? Find out by looking in the phone book under your state's Department of Labor and calling.

Does your church or religious group have a support group where unemployed parents can share resources and strategies? Does your local Y or community center have any free seminars on job seeking or low-cost child care for younger brothers and sisters?

And don't forget your local library . . . a great resource for free help. Ask your librarian to help you locate some books you can check out and take home. Some topics to inquire about are resumé writing, job-seeking strategies, local businesses, and careers.

A Positive Attitude

Your unemployed parent can really benefit from keeping a positive attitude, but this can be hard to do. You can help your parent and yourself by trying to keep up your own positive attitude. You may feel that fun is not in the budget right now. But there are many pleasurable things you can do for free—a walk in the park, a bicycle ride with friends, a good book from the library. Make a list of fun things you can do by yourself, with your friends, and with your family.

Share the Workload

Help with household chores. Experts say that looking for work can be more exhausting than working at a job. Your unemployed parent will be grateful for any help you can provide. Can you cook, do the laundry, baby-sit a younger brother or sister? Use your imagination, and you'll find you can really help a lot.

And remember, it's not just what you do . . . it's how you do it. Remain as cheerful as you can and let your parents know you are helping them because you love them, not because you have to.

Your unemployed parent will probably welcome the assistance, if you can do any household chores.

CHAPTER 7

Special Issues

Q My dad goes out every day to look for work. But when he comes home, I can smell liquor on his breath. I'm really scared that something terrible is going to happen. What should I do?

A It's natural for you to feel scared. It sounds like your dad may have a drinking problem. If that's the case, only he can solve it. But if his problem is affecting you—and it seems to be—you must get some help for yourself. Alateen is a group that you should know about. They have free support groups all over the country. Alateen is for teenagers who don't have drinking problems themselves, but who are close to someone who does. The other teens you'll meet at Alateen are going through problems similar to yours, with their parents who have drinking problems. At Alateen, you'll get useful advice about dealing with your particular situation. See the "Where to Go for Help" section at the back of this book for more information about Alateen and other places where you can find help.

• • • • • • • • • • •

We have discussed already how losing a job can be damaging for a parent. We have seen how unemployment changes a parent's self-image and the way he or she interacts with the whole family. Now we'll talk about some of the extreme negative consequences that can result from unemployment.

Substance Abuse

When people lose jobs, they lose more than money. They often lose all the good feelings they had about themselves. Frequently, parents in this situation feel like failures, and they try to cope with the negative feelings in ways that hurt them. Some people try to escape from the bad feelings by drinking or by using drugs. If your parent is drinking too much or abusing drugs, consider the following questions:

■ Do you hide your real feelings and pretend you don't care?

■ Do you tell lies to cover up for your parent's drinking or odd behavior?

■ Do you stay out of your house as much as possible because you hate being there?

■ Are you afraid to upset your parent because you fear it will set off a drinking or drug binge?

■ Do you make threats such as, "If you don't stop drinking, I'll run away"?

If you answered "yes" to any of these questions, your problems may be too complicated for you to handle alone. Help is available—your other parent, a relative, a school counselor, Alateen. Get help now.

When Your House Is Not Your Home

Domestic violence—violence within the family—happens in homes throughout the country. It occurs in rich families, poor families, urban families, rural families, and families of all religious backgrounds.

In addition to physically suffering from such abuse, victims of domestic violence often blame themselves for the abuse. Victims may believe that they provoked the abuse—either because the abuser says so or because they feel guilty. Victims of physical abuse must try to realize that they are never responsible for this violent behavior. They should have no feelings of guilt.

Unemployment is a stressful situation that may bring out violent behavior in a parent who previously was not abusive. Or it may cause a parent who was strict and harsh before the unemployment to cross the line into actual abuse. No matter why your parent is abusing you—if this is the case—it is not OK. There is no excuse for anyone abusing you. Ask yourself the following questions:

■ Are you afraid to talk to your parent because you fear it will provoke physical abuse?

■ Have you ever concealed or lied about the bruises inflicted by your parent?

■ Do you believe there is no one who could possibly understand how you feel?

■ Have you considered calling the police about your parent's behavior?

If you answered "yes" to any of these questions, you need to get help to end the abusive situation that exists in your home. If you haven't tried talking to your nonabusive parent, try doing so now. Be as specific as you can. But if this is not an option in your situation, talk to an adult you feel you can trust—a teacher, guidance counselor, coach. Or call one of the toll-free hot lines listed in the "Where to Go for Help" section at the back of this book.

Desertion

Sometimes unemployed parents feel such tremendous guilt about failing their families that they actually run away from the situation and desert the family they love. Hector had that sad experience and shared his feelings about it.

"My father worked for the same company for ten years. Then the boss's son took it over, and they fired half the people. Laid off, they said. But I say the guy just got rid of the people who had worked for his old man and brought in a bunch of his friends. Then the troubles really started.

"My parents were never one of those happy couples you see on TV, but I guess they were kind of happy. I mean, they had arguments and stuff, but nothing serious. When my dad lost his job I thought he'd get a new one right away. I mean, he was a hard worker and all. But he kept coming home from interviews saying that they wanted younger guys who they could pay less. He sort of gave up and stopped looking.

"He and Mom started arguing real bad, saying terrible things to each other. The fights got worse, and I started spending a lot of time at my friend's house . . . I just couldn't stand being home. So I come home one day and my mother is throwing Dad's things in the garbage. I was totally freaked out and asked her what she was doing. She just started crying. Then my sister told me that my dad left that day, while we were in school. He didn't even leave a note . . . nothing. Mom found out from a friend of his that he said he's never coming back. She said that he was really running from himself, not from us. But from where I sit, it sure looks like he left us."

Parents who desert their families may or may not return. Either way, if it happens to you, you need to move on with your life. To do this, you will most likely need help. Talk to your other parent—you are both probably feeling a lot of the same things. If the parent who deserted tries to contact you, even though you're very angry, talk to him or her if you can.

Divorce: A House Divided

Sometimes other bad feelings come to the surface when a parent loses a job, straining the marriage, and causing divorce. Even though divorce is fairly common in the United States today, it is rough being the child of divorced or divorcing parents. It's difficult to deal with the angry feelings your parents may have toward each other, which may extend to you and your brothers and sisters. You may feel guilty—that somehow you are responsible for their divorce. Many young people whose parents are getting divorced feel that it is their fault that their family is breaking up. This is untrue, and it's important for you to remember that parents separate because of their problems with each other, not because of their kids.

If your parents are divorcing, here are some other important points for you to remember:

■ You don't have to choose sides; you can still love them both. If one parent tries to win your allegiance by turning you against the other, tell him or her that you love them both and that you don't want to be caught in the middle by taking sides with one or the other.

■ Talk to your parents about your needs and feelings. They may be so involved in their own problems that they are overlooking yours.

■ You can survive your parents' divorce. Yes, it's painful, but look around you. Many kids have survived divorce, and you will, too.

■ And, of course, help is available. There's no need to handle this alone. The hot lines listed in the "Where to Go for Help" section can help you find a trained counselor or a support group in your community.

Homelessness

Homelessness is a serious problem in this country. Recent studies suggest that families make up 30 to 40 percent of the homeless population in America. According to some experts, 500,000 to 700,000 children are currently homeless.

Some of these families become homeless because a parent has lost a job. Families that have recently become homeless as a result of unemployment may move around a lot. They may stay with different friends or relatives, or they may live in special shelters. Homelessness creates many problems for families, one of which is the disruption in schooling for the children.

Jill is a teen from a homeless family, and she told what it's like. "Me and my family have been homeless for about a year . . . since my mother lost her job. For a while we stayed with my

Maximum Monthly Food Stamp Allotments, 1992	
Household size	48 states and D.C.*
1 person	$111
2 persons	$203
3 persons	$292
4 persons	$370
5 persons	$440
6 persons	$529

*Allotments in Alaska and Hawaii are slightly higher.

Source: U.S. Department of Agriculture.

Families may apply for food stamps at local welfare offices. Eligibility is based on family size and income.

aunt. But my brothers were always fighting with her kids, and anyway she said she felt bad and all because she couldn't afford to support us. We bounced around the shelters for a while and that was pretty bad. Lots of families jammed together. Babies crying all the time and kids fighting. We had to watch our stuff because people would steal stuff in the shelter.

"It was really hard to get any sleep, and school was real far away. I had to take a bus every day. It was hard enough being in a new school. But the regular kids there, they didn't want anything to do with us 'shelter kids,' so I was on my own.

"Now we live in a motel. It's supposed to be a move up from the shelter. It's not a regular motel because it's mostly filled up with other homeless families. But it's a little better than the shelter. We can't cook though because there's no kitchen.

"My mom is in a training program now to teach her a new kind of job. I sure hope it works out, because it's terrible being homeless . . . you know, not having your own place."

Homelessness is an extremely unsettling experience, but usually temporary. Remember that even though you don't have a home right now, you do have a family. There are community programs to help homeless kids and their families. If your family needs a place to live or other assistance, check your local telephone directory under all of the following headings to find an agency that can help you:

- community services
- housing
- social services
- welfare
- mental health
- government agencies

You can also call any local Y, United Way, community center, the Salvation Army, or any church or synagogue.

Parental unemployment will cause some changes in your life. We've tried to give you an idea of the range of problems that may occur and provide some practical strategies for coping if they do.

What Is Welfare?

During the 1930s, President Franklin Roosevelt introduced legislation aimed at easing the distress caused by the Great Depression.

The Social Security Act of 1935 was one of the most important laws passed during that period. One section of the act established a program of aid to dependent children. It was called Aid to Families with Dependent Children (AFDC) and is the program that most often comes to mind when we speak of "welfare."

There is no single unified welfare program in the United States. Most are joint federal-state programs in which the federal contribution varies, depending on the wealth of the state.

Who Receives Welfare?

For many years, AFDC was limited to families in which a child was deprived of parental care or support because of death, disability, or continued absence of the parent from the home. In 1961, Congress expanded the program to provide AFDC to two-parent families if a parent had a recent work history, but was then unemployed. The program currently covers two-parent families in which the principal earner—mother or father—is unemployed.

Participation in Other Programs

AFDC enrollment automatically qualifies a family for Medicaid coverage. Medicaid is a federally funded medical assistance program. Families receiving AFDC can also apply for training under the Job Training Partnership Act (JTPA). States may also grant AFDC families automatic eligibility for the Low-Income Home Energy Assistance Program (LIHEAP).

Average Monthly AFDC Payment for a Family of Four

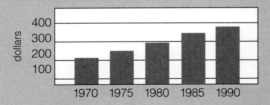

Source: Family Support Administration and the Congressional Research Service.

The purpose of welfare is to help families with dependent children meet an immediate financial need. It is intended to be a temporary solution until the family becomes self-sufficient and financially independent.

Where to Go for Help

There are currently no national organizations that specifically deal with teenagers whose parents are unemployed. Even so, help is available. A trained counselor or therapist can help with any problems that you or your family are experiencing. Your school will have a guidance counselor, a psychologist, or a social worker to help you or to refer you to a trained specialist in your community. You can look in the phone book under your state's Department of Labor to locate your local unemployment office. Your parent may have been to this office already to apply for unemployment benefits. Ask an unemployment counselor there if there are any support groups in your area for teens of unemployed parents. You should also check with your librarian, church, synagogue, or community center to find out about local support groups.

There are many support groups and treatment centers that deal with the specific problems that you or family members might be experiencing—such as alcoholism, drug abuse, domestic violence. Whatever your problem, one of the organizations listed below can probably guide you toward the appropriate group in your community. Help is available—don't be afraid to ask for it!

National Organizations

Alcohol and Drug Problems
  Association of North America
1101 15th Street, NW, Suite 204
Washington, DC 20005
  This organization will send you information on alcohol and drug problems. Enclose a stamped self-addressed envelope with your request.

Boys Town (800) 448-3000
  Don't let the name of this organization fool you. You can call whether you are female or male. Boys Town can help you in two important ways. A trained counselor will talk to you about any problem you have.

The counselor can also refer you to services in your area, such as support groups or counseling. Don't worry about the cost. The call to Boys Town is toll-free, and the community services they recommend are free or have fees based on a sliding scale, which means you pay what you can afford to pay.

National Self-Help
  Clearinghouse
25 West 43rd Street, Room 620
New York, New York 10036
  The National Self-Help Clearinghouse can provide information on self-help

groups throughout the country. They prefer that you write, rather than phone. Write a brief letter explaining your problem and be sure to enclose a stamped self-addressed envelope. They will send you a list of self-help groups in your area.

United Way
Check your local telephone white pages or yellow pages (under Social Services) for the United Way office near you. They will refer you to the appropriate agency.

Hot Lines
Al-Anon Family Groups (Canada)
(613) 722-1830

Alateen (800) 344-2666
If you don't have a problem with alcohol, but someone close to you does, you need to know about Alateen. Like AA, they have free support groups. Call their toll-free number for the group nearest you.

Alcoholics Anonymous (AA)
You may already know about this long-established support group for alcoholics. AA is the group that actually started the whole self-help movement. If you feel that you or your parent has a drinking problem, you should find out more about AA. The meetings are free and as the name says, anonymous. That means that the meetings are private and confidential. Look under Alcoholics Anonymous in the phone book.

The Center for Substance Abuse Treatment (800) 662-4357
If you think your parent may have an alcohol or drug abuse problem, you can call this toll-free number for information about groups in your area.

Children's Aid Society (Canada)
(613) 733-0670

National Clearinghouse on Alcohol and Drug Information (800) 729-6686
Call this toll-free number for free information—reports, pamphlets, and posters—about alcohol and drugs.

The Nineline (800) 999-9999

Youth Crisis Hot Line
(800) 448-4663
You can call the two toll-free numbers listed above anytime—24 hours a day, 7 days a week—and discuss any problem at all. Trained counselors will talk with you directly or refer you to help in your community.

Youth Services Bureau (Canada)
(613) 729-1000

For More Information

Articles

Flint, Jerry. "Keep a Resumé on the Floppy, but Don't Panic." *Forbes.* April 26, 1993.

Harrison, Ann. "Laid Off, Laid Low: How to Beat the Unemployment Blues." *American Health Magazine.* September 1991.

Levine, Karen. "What to Do If You're Fired: Job Loss and the Family." *Parents Magazine.* February 1990.

"The New Unemployed." *Fortune.* March 8, 1993.

Rosenblatt, Roger. "Out of Work in America." *Life Magazine.* August 1991.

Books

An asterisk (*) indicates Young Adult book.

*Booher, Dianna Daniels. *Help! We're Moving.* Julian Messner, 1983.

*Carlson, Dale. *Boys Have Feelings Too.* Atheneum, 1980.

Cetron, Marvin. *The Great Job Shake-Out: How to Find a Career After the Crash.* Simon and Schuster, 1988.

*Gilbert, Sara. *Trouble at Home.* Lothrop, Lee & Shepard, 1981.

*Johnson, Eric W. *How to Live with Parents and Teachers.* Westminster Press, 1986.

*Lang, Denise V. *But Everyone Else Looks So Sure of Themselves.* Shoe Tree Press, 1991.

Leman, Kevin. *Keeping Your Family Together When the World Is Falling Apart.* Delacorte, 1992.

*McMillian, Daniel. *Winning the Battle Against Drugs: Rehabilitation Programs.* Franklin Watts, 1991.

Moreau, Daniel. *Take Charge of Your Career.* Kiplinger Books, 1990.

*Ryan, Elizabeth A. *Straight Talk About Parents.* Facts on File, 1989.

Secunda, Victoria. *When You and Your Mother Can't Be Friends.* Delacorte Press, 1990.

Snelling, Robert, and Anne Snelling. *Jobs!* Fireside Books, 1992.

Sokol, Julia, and Steven Carter. *Lives Without Balance.* Random House, 1992.

Tepper, Ron. *Power Resumes.* John Wiley, and Sons, 1992.

INDEX